PHOTOGRAPHIC
PAPER

Taking Photographs

by Lynne Anderson

Table of Contents

What Is Photography?

Do you enjoy looking at pictures of yourself or your family and friends? Taking and looking at **photographs** can be lots of fun! The art of taking photographs is called **photography**.

Americans take more than 20 billion photographs every year.

Photographs are pictures that form on a surface that is sensitive to light. They are taken with a device called a **camera**.

There are many kinds of cameras. Some cameras need light-sensitive paper called **film** to form an image. After a picture is taken, the film is **developed** to make the photographs you are familiar with.

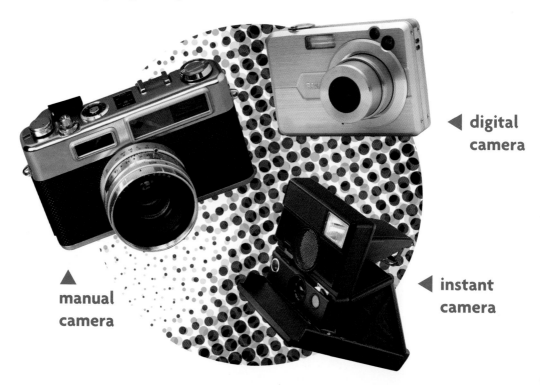

◀ digital camera

▲ manual camera

◀ instant camera

Other cameras can give you a finished photo just moments after you take a picture. The images are developed right inside the camera!

Cameras called digital cameras let you take a picture and download it to a computer. These cameras are also called filmless cameras—they don't need any film or developing time to take and make pictures!

Did You Know?

The first photograph was taken in the early 1800s. Back then, cameras and photographs were much different than they are

today. Photographs were very expensive and difficult to make. It could take almost thirty minutes to snap a single photo! Most people took photographs on special occasions only—maybe just once or twice in their lives!

A camera is a box that lets in light through a small opening, or hole. This is true no matter what kind of camera it is. A **shutter** covers the hole. It opens and closes when you take a picture.

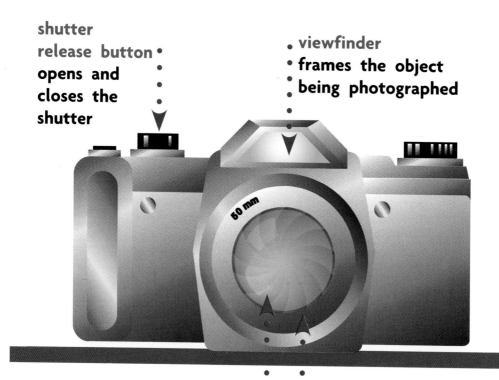

shutter release button •
opens and closes the shutter

• viewfinder
frames the object being photographed

50 mm

shutter • • • • • • • • • •
controls the amount of light that enters the camera

• lens
focuses the image being photographed

The shutter controls the amount of light that enters the camera. When the shutter is open, light shines onto a light-sensitive surface, such as film, in the back of the camera. An image forms on this surface.

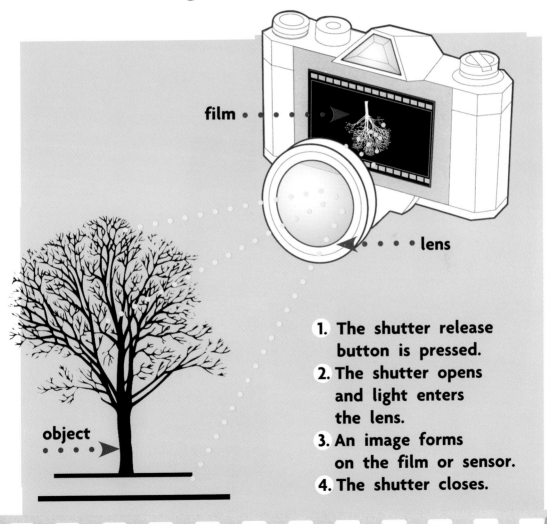

film

lens

object

1. The shutter release button is pressed.
2. The shutter opens and light enters the lens.
3. An image forms on the film or sensor.
4. The shutter closes.

How Do You Make a Pinhole Camera?

You can make a simple camera called a **pinhole camera**. A pinhole camera is a box that lets in light through a pinhole. When photographic paper is placed in the box, you can use the box to take a photograph.

These photos were taken with a pinhole camera.

Photographic paper is a special type of paper that is coated with chemicals. These chemicals make the paper sensitive to light. When light hits the surface of the paper, an image forms on the paper. The paper needs to be developed so that you can see the image, or picture. This process needs to be done in a photography store that has a **darkroom**.

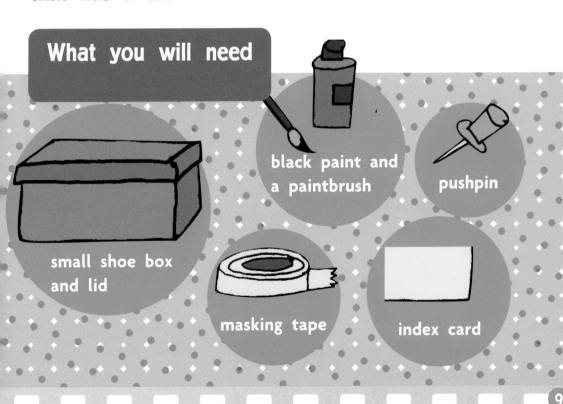

What you will need

black paint and a paintbrush

pushpin

small shoe box and lid

masking tape

index card

Step 1 Paint the inside of the shoe box and lid black. Set them aside to dry.

Step 2 When the paint has dried, use a pushpin to gently make a hole in the box. Put the hole in the center of the long side of the box. Make sure to make only one hole!

Step 3 Put the lid on the box. Then tape
an index card to the lid to cover the
pinhole. This is your camera's shutter.
Use only one piece of tape. Place it
across the top of the index card so that the
card can be easily lifted like a flap.

Your pinhole camera is done! Now
all you need to do is load it with
photographic paper, and you're ready
to take a picture.

How Do You Load a Pinhole Camera?

Before you can use your pinhole camera, you will have to load it with photographic paper.

What you will need

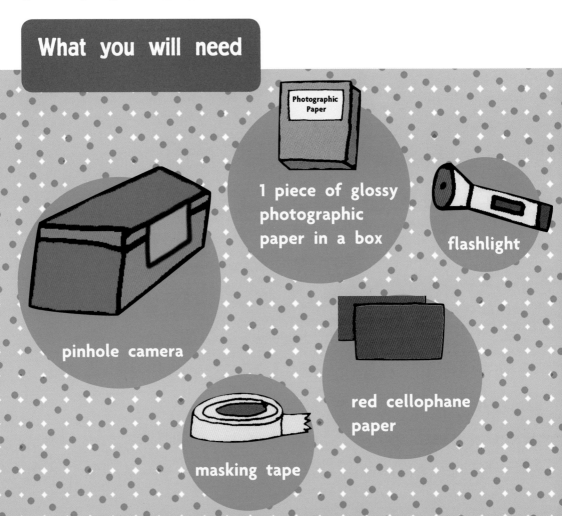

1 piece of glossy photographic paper in a box

flashlight

pinhole camera

red cellophane paper

masking tape

Step 1 Make a **safelight** by taping
two sheets of red cellophane
paper over the light end of a flashlight.

▲ A safelight is a special light that photographers
use when working with photographic paper or
film. This special light lets photographers see
but does not affect the paper or film.

The following steps must be done in a dark room. For the best results, you should use a room that has no windows, such as a closet. Use your safelight to help you see.

Step 2 Remove the piece of photographic paper from the box. Cut the paper so that it fits inside the pinhole camera.

Step 3 Place the paper inside the camera on the side opposite the pinhole. The glossy side should face the pinhole. Tape the top two corners in place.

Step 4 While you are still in the dark room, put the lid on the camera. If the lid does not fit tightly, tape it in place so that light cannot enter the box.

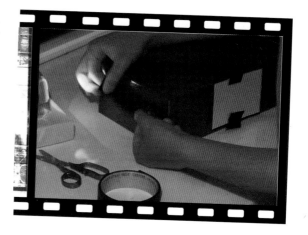

How Do You Take a Photograph With a Pinhole Camera?

Step 1 Put the pinhole camera in a sunny spot. The shutter should face the object you wish to photograph. For the best results, choose a faraway object that does not move.

What you will need

- loaded pinhole camera
- masking tape
- box for your photographic paper
- place to have your photographic paper developed

Step 2 Now lift the shutter and tape it to the box. Leave the camera in place for three to five minutes.

Step 3 Then remove the tape and let the shutter return to its original position.

Step 4 Take your camera back into the dark room. Remove the lid from the camera. Take out the photographic paper and put it back into the box.

Step 5 Take the photographic paper to a photography store to be developed. Remember to keep the paper in its box. When the paper is developed, you will see an image.

You can use your pinhole camera again and again. Just load it with a new piece of photographic paper each time you want to take a picture.

How well does your camera work? Experiment with your camera and photography by taking pictures of a variety of things.

Glossary

camera (KA-mer-uh): a device that can take photographs

darkroom (DARK-room): a room with special lighting that is used when photographers work with light-sensitive paper

develop (dih-VEL-up): to treat photographic paper or film with special chemicals so that the picture can be seen

film (FILM): a material coated with a substance that changes when light hits it

photograph (FOH-tuh-graf): a picture formed on a surface that is sensitive to light

photography (fuh-TAH-gruh-fee): the art of taking photographs

pinhole camera (PIN-hole KA-mer-uh): a camera that lets in light through a pinhole

safelight (SAFE-lite): a special light used when working with photographic paper or film

shutter (SHUH-ter): a movable cover over a camera lens that controls the amount of light that enters the camera

Index